Lars Rasmussen

WHAT CAN BUDDHA TEACH THE RAIN?

Lars Rasmussen

WHAT CAN BUDDHA TEACH THE RAIN?

Twenty Poems to Han-shan
and Seventy Poems Ascribed to Him

SERVING HOUSE BOOKS

What Can Buddha Teach the Rain?
Twenty Poems to Han-shan
and Seventy Poems Ascribed to Him

Copyright © 2010 Lars Rasmussen

All rights reserved.

No part of this book may be used or reproduced in any manner whatsoever without the prior written permission of the copyright holder except for brief quotations in critical articles or reviews.

Cover art by Lars Rasmussen

Author photo by Birte Gerner Larsson

Serving House Books logo by Barry Lereng Wilmont

ISBN: 978-0-9826921-5-8

Published by Serving House Books

www.servinghousebooks.com

First Serving House Books Edition 2010

CONTENTS

9	There Never Was a Poet Called Han-shan
	I. Poems to Han-shan
13	Man and Mountain
13	Flea
13	Rock
14	Warnings Against Han-shan
15	Meeting the Man
16	Equipment
16	On Top of Mount Han-shan
17	Riding the Tiger
17	Han-shan Is Here
17	One Plus One Is One
18	The Road to Han-shan
21	Questioning Han-shan's Skull
25	Odd Man
25	Poets in Debate
25	Monsoon
26	Questions
26	Ascent
26	The Spider and the Moon
27	The Merry Executioners
29	Death of Han-shan
	II. Poems Ascribed to Han-shan
33	Shih-te
33	Shadow
33	In the Snow
34	Han-shan and the Tiger
35	Toad
35	Geometry
35	Han-shan's Cat (I)
36	Han-shan's Cat (II)

36	Oracle Bones
36	Tiger Script
37	Hush!
37	Perspective
37	Han-shan Blues
38	The Torch Dragon
38	Weight
39	Crow
39	What Can Buddha Teach the Rain?
40	Han-shan's Cat (III)
40	Enlightenment
40	Pond
41	Threat
41	Evening
42	Exposed in a Dream
42	Han-shan's Cat (IV)
42	Perfect Day
43	The Clouds
43	Making an End of It
43	Han-shan's Cat (V)
44	Clay
44	Kingfishers
44	Dreaming of Spring
44	Qin
45	Searching for Mount Han-shan
46	Night Picture
46	Han-shan's Cat (VI)
46	Han-shan's Cat (VII)
47	Han-shan's Cat (VIII)
47	Thank the Fish
48	Balls
48	Egg
48	In Shih-te's Hut
49	To the Court Poets
49	The Moon and the Eye
50	Hare
50	Misty Night
51	Words

51	Rat
51	Footprints
52	The Wind
52	Spider
53	Ti-tsang's Children
55	Shih-te Bows Out
56	Shih-te's Death
56	Hut and Castle
56	Trouble
57	End of Mount Han-shan
57	Response
57	Mosquitos
58	Ageing
58	Cow and Abbot
58	Tiger Trap
59	Bowl
59	Melting Snow
59	Measuring the Mountain
60	Isolation
60	Speaking to the Dead
60	Catch a Cloud
61	Moon
61	Something That Looks Like a Cow
62	Moss
64	Imagining His Last Poem
64	Wind at the Door
65	Han-shan's Jisei
66	Appendix I: Bone and Marrow
68	Appendix II: Han-shan's Proverbs
69	Notes

LARS RASMUSSEN

Lars Rasmussen is a man of many parts: He has owned and managed an antiquarian bookshop in the center of Copenhagen, The Booktrader, for over twenty years now. As a publisher, he has issued excellent and rare works on South African jazz, golf and other topics as well as a CD recording series which includes both jazz and many of the greatest living poets in Denmark. And he has published many books of his own stories, not to mention his annual Christmas journal containing fiction, poems, essays, and art by many of his customers—and he does have some impressive customers who include writers, musicians, artists, singers, actors, journalists, professors, and most of all—readers.

THERE NEVER WAS A POET CALLED HAN-SHAN

There never was a T'ang poet called Han-shan. That's why we had to invent him.

To me it is clear that Han-shan is a persona invented by Lu Ch'iu-Yin, the late 9th century compiler of the first Han-shan anthology. The motif of the mountain hermit cum poet occurs frequently in T'ang poetry, the most notable example being a poem by Po-Chü-i, translated by Arthur Waley as *Madly Singing in the Mountains*. I believe Lu Ch'iu-Yin was inspired by this romantic motif to compose his anthology himself, perhaps with the help of a few friends, and that composing Han-shan poetry - that is, rude T'ang pastiches attributed to this fictional author - then became a popular passtime among Chinese poets. This view is supported by the fact that up to this date no research has been able to provide any examples of Han-shan's poetry, nor any historic or literary references to the man as such, predating Lu Ch'iu-Yin's anthology. Arthur Waley calls Han-shan a state of mind, one might also call him a literary style.

The many artistic depictions, Chinese and Japanese, of Han-shan and his friend Shih-te (usually depicted as a look-alike) are inspired by Lu Ch'iu-Yin's introduction to his anthology. From this fairytale-like text, itself about as famous as the poems, comes the conception, clearly reflected in the paintings, of Han-shan as a madman, the archetypal fool on the hill. The poems themselves definitely (and disappointingly) reveal not the slightest sign of madness.

Even if somebody one day should succeed in pointing out a historic person whose life and activities have given birth to the legend of Han-shan, there is little guarantee that this person actually wrote a single one of the 300 poems now ascribed to him, and he would hardly be able to recognize himself in the picture we try to paint of him. It is like comparing the historic Bishop Nicholas of Myra to the Santa Claus we made him into.

Han-shan is a poetic invention - and a good one, it seems, since 'his' poetry is being read, translated and re-translated to this day. Likewise, at least in Japan and China, artists are still fond of making depictions of his foolishly grinning face.

A legend he is. What makes him so interesting? For me, it is not the bulk of poems. Much of what they say has been better expressed by other Chinese poets and the persona who speaks in the Han-shan poems often seems vain, self-referential and self-defensive. No, I am not fascinated by the Han-shan poems, I am fascinated by the myth of Han-shan.

Han-shan means Cold Mountain and the man Han-shan supposedly took his name after the mountain Han-shan, in Southern China, on which he chose to live. Was he naming himself after a mountain because he had a big ego or, contrarily, because he had reached a state of no-ego and thus become one with his surroundings? While some of the poems suggest the former, I of course go for the latter. I imagine Han-shan as a person who has become whole to such a degree that he is not only one with himself - that is: has integrated all parts of his personality - has no shadow, as our friends the Jungians would put it - he is also one with his surroundings. He doesn't fear the wild animals, he doesn't fear karma or destiny, he does not want to prove anything, he does not want to achieve anything, he rests completely within himself and allows open space for all sorts of flaws and inconsistensies in his character.

This is my Han-shan; now show me yours.

—Lars Rasmussen

To get yourself a good Han-shan collection, you need to buy the two complete translations of the poems (not that they differ alarmingly): *Collected Songs of Cold Mountain,* translated by Red Pine, Copper Canyon Press, 2000, *The Poetry of Han-shan,* translated by Robert G. Henricks, State University Of New York Press, 1990, Burton Watson's translation of 100 poems, *Cold Mountain. 100 Poems by the T'ang Poet Han-shan,* Jonathan Cape, 1962, Arthur Waley's translation of 27 poems in *Encounter,* Vol. III, no. 3, 1954, Arthur Tobias' translation of 34 poems in *The View from Cold Mountain,* White Pine Press, 1982, JP Seaton's translation of 95 poems in *Cold Mountain Poems,* Shambhala, 2009, Gary Snyder's translation of 24 poems (and, importantly, including Po-Ch'iu-Yin's introduction to the first Han-shan anthology) in *Evergreen Review,* Vol. II, no. 6, 1958, reprinted in *The Evergreen Review Reader,* Grove Press, 1968, and in *Anthology of Chinese Literature,* edited by Cyril Birch, Penguin Books 1965 (one of few Chinese anthologies in English to include Han-shan), plus a copy of Jack Kerouac's *Dharma Bums.* Check also books on Chinese and Japanese art, especially ink painting, for visual representations of Han-shan and Shih-te, or do a Google picture search.

I. POEMS TO HAN-SHAN

MAN AND MOUNTAIN

A mop of hair
and a broom in hand,
big fat lips
framing a silly grin,
uttering not much more
than a *Ho!* and a *Ha!*
Did he ever wash?
Did he ever change his clothes?
What made him call himself a mountain?

FLEA

I call myself Han-shan
and yet I am nothing
but a flea,
happily jumping about
on the back of the true Han-shan.

ROCK

If I only had a mountain,
like Han-shan,
I would carve my words in rock.
But living in the lowlands
I am forced to write upon the wind.

WARNINGS AGAINST HAN-SHAN

Don't walk up Mount Han-shan.
You'll find a madman living there.
He doesn't know his place in this world.
He spends the day carving wooden Buddhas
and the evening feeding them to the fire.
He'll bring a hare to the tiger's den,
thinking he has found him a friend.
He once cut a warbler free of a giant spider's web,
just to serve it to his cat.
He'll climb the tallest pine tree
in an attempt to dust off the moon.
He mistakes the temple for a whorehouse
and makes indecent proposals to the nuns.
He doesn't know the difference between big and small.
He thinks the mountain is a hump on his back
and he once dug a hole and tried to bury the moon.
He cracks *koans* like walnuts
and thinks himself wiser than Buddha,
yet he dares to wipe his ass with holy sutras
and would never dream of entering Nirvana.
He'll eat raw meat if the tiger invites him.
He'll roast a phoenix,
sleep in an ant hill,
try to kiss the morning sun.
Don't walk up Mount Han-shan.
You'll find a madman living there.
He'll get you drunk with madness
and you'll never find yourself sober again.

MEETING THE MAN

I wanted to meet Han-shan
so I packed my things and left my home
to seek him out. But first I had to fight my way
up the mountain that bears his name.

It took days. Bleeding and exhausted,
I stumbled through the mist,
seeking him in caves and thickets,
shouting out his name:
Han-shan! Do you hear me?

When at last I got clear of the clouds
and walked out in the light of day,
I met him face to face.

The bastard grinned at me so foolishly
while uttering some silly *Ho*'s and *Ha*'s
that I could think of nothing better than to smack him.
Yes, to kick him! And to wipe him off the face
of that mountain he called his.

I threw a rock in his face - *Ouch!*
and - *Whack!* he hit me with his broom
We wrestled for how many hours I don't recall
through the rest of the day and all through the following night
until finally this morning when the sun rose,
I found myself alone on the slope.

What happened to the other?

I sit on the top of Han-shan mountain
right outside the cave that was his
and wonder: Am I really me?

And have I thrown that demon Han-shan off,
off of his beloved mountain? Killed him perhaps?
Or am I Han-shan,
having successfully disposed of me?

EQUIPMENT

I want the voice of Po Chü-i
and the brush of Fa Ch'ang.
Bring me the glasses of Chuang Tsu,
and Han-shan,
will you lend me your broom?

ON TOP OF MOUNT HAN-SHAN

Standing on top of Mount Han-shan
I decide to dust my broom

The warm southern wind is blowing
The sky is clear of clouds
My cock points to the sky and explodes

As I watch my sperm fall freely
well over 5,000 feet
I shout to all corners of the world:

This is how I fertilize the earth
This is how the ocean is born

RIDING THE TIGER

Riding along on the back
of Han-shan's tiger.
These are the paths he followed,
this was his cave,
these are his clouds,
his sky, his mountain.
These footprints
could be his,
and behind this cliff
is where he used to shit.
I am as close to him
as one man can be to another.
Was *he* too plagued by fleas?

HAN-SHAN IS HERE

Why go to China
to search for Han-shan
when he is here,
right outside your door,
lying dead drunk in the gutter?

ONE PLUS ONE IS ONE

There cannot be two persons
in this world.
If he is one
I must be him.

THE ROAD TO HAN-SHAN

The road to Mount Han-shan has been trodden by few
even though it isn't steep.
I start my ascent with no ambition of reaching the top,
but to seek out the tracks of those who went before me
and see where and why they gave up.

Some are more lazy than others,
their characters weak, low their ambitions.
Barely have I walked an hour,
before the first piece of evidence appears:
a broken bottle marks the place
where *Jack Kerouac* gave up,
for lack of booze.
I've had it, he said.
This is not the road I want to follow.
Besides, my shoes are worn
and I need to go back after booze.

The road gets tougher, and I sit down by a brook for a rest.
Right beside me, I notice a workman's cap lie discarded.
This is where *Chairman Mao* swore off.
This road leads nowhere, the big man exclaimed,
and how will the masses ever benefit from such an uninviting place?
One day I'll have the revolutionary guard return
and flatten this useless hill.
So great is the power of the thousands.

Higher yet, and only steeper gets the path.
Sweat runs into my eyes when suddenly
the blinding sun reveals another sign,
a single *aum*, carved deep in a cliff,
marking, of course, where *Lord Buddha* thought it enough.
How can one preach the law of the wheel
where no wheel can ever roll?

Excuse enough, I guess,
for the grand man to turn around.

The higher I scale, the finer relics I find.
Hours have passed with no observations
when, spread out on a flatbed rock,
my eye detects the scattered remains
of a bundle of broken straws.
This is where *the diviner* gave up.
How can one read the Book of Changes
where stalks of milfoil won't grow?
And besides, on a mountain top,
who needs to know the future?

Fewer and fewer are the signs of human presence,
and tougher and tougher the path.
I'm about to stop my ascent and turn around
when, posed on a rock,
the finest, tiniest litter catches my eye:
a broken, greyish cocoon signals
that this is where *Chuang Tsu* woke up from his dream
of being a human, quickly dried his wings,
and fluttered off to the flowerbed valley below.
Who wants to be a butterfly
on a cold mountain where no flower will grow?

Above me now, the peak lies covered in clouds.
This is where my quest should stop.
What remains is home to wild beasts only.
Already I hear the tigers roar,
and the eagle is seen guarding his nest.
The air is thin, the ground is barren,
how could any man ever have walked
such unhomely slopes?
My conclusion is clear:
Han-shan, the man, is a myth,
an invention, a romantic poet's dream.

Yet I decide to continue up through the clouds,
if not for anything else, then at least for the view.

Clear of the clouds, I can see forever.
Stunning views unfold in all directions,
to the south the ocean, reflecting the sun,
to the east, the west and the north,
widespread valleys and rolling hills abound.
It strikes me I could be the first human
ever to enjoy these wonderous sights.

The day is waning and it is time to get back.
I turn around and suddenly,
exposed in the light of the setting sun,
an unexpected sight appears.
A heap of human dung,
piled up next to that of a tiger,
says as much as this: *Han-shan was here.*
The legend is true:
a man can relieve himself
of the burden of human relations,
cut the bonds of family and friends,
forget his own name, discard his gods,
move to a mountain
and become one with the wild.
My heart is beating.
Is he still here?
The dung seems fresh,
yet I lack the courage to stay.
This mountain is his,
and I am a mere intruder, not strong enough
to live the solitary life of a hermit.
Besides, a single mountain cannot hold two of his kind.
I have to leave it to him.
Humbly I step back
and let myself disappear into the clouds.

QUESTIONING HAN-SHAN'S SCULL

Searching for relics
on the slopes of Mount Han-shan,
one morning I stumble upon a broadly grinning scull,
half buried in a bed of emerald moss.
Deformed at the brow,
the face is so strangely looking
that it must have belonged to some retard.
Browned and brittled, it seems to have been lying here
for how many hundred years I can't tell.
But where is the skeleton to which it belonged?
No other bones are seen near it.
The scull must have dropped from the upper slopes,
perhaps when a tiger, in ancient time,
tore it off its body. A fascinating relic indeed.
As I break it loose from the ground,
a toad sends an angry look
before reluctantly leaving its burrow
dug out underneath the jaw.
I brush the cranium clean of soil and moss,
then lift it up to inspect it in the light,
trying to imagine how it looked
when once it was covered with flesh and skin.
The thought suddenly strikes me:
It is Han-shan, no doubt!
This is my best find ever, my chance of a lifetime
to get near the man I admire.
Quickly I hide the scull in my rucksack
and hurry home. My plan is clear:
I want to make the cranium speak.
Soul will meet soul, like it has never happened before.

Back home, I lock the door carefully behind me.
Holding the scull up in front of me,
staring into its two empty eyes,
I get overcome by doubt.

Not knowing the long lost recipes
that in ancient times enabled the alchemists to revive the dead,
how can I perform a proper invocation
of the soul that once inhabited this dead bone?
It strikes me I may as well give up,
when suddenly a stir goes through the scull,
the jaw begins to move, and a loud moan escapes it:
        Where am I?
Trembling, I shout out: *Han-shan, is it you?*
        Says the scull: I am me, of course, but who are you?
        And why do you disturb my peace?
An admirer. I know I may be rude,
but I have brought you here to question you
about a few simple things I need to know.
Tell me first: How is it to be dead?
Have you been reborn since that time, so long ago,
when you wrote those poems I admire?
Or have you been living like a ghost?
        No rebirth. A silly lie.
        The dead reside in a world of their own,
        a world of no changes,
        so much better than that of the living.
        No hell, no paradise,
        just a world of no will,
        where nothing is good or evil.
        But why do you ask? The day may soon enough come
        for you to enter the world of the dead.
True. But what about the words of Buddha? Are they wrong
or do they simply not mean a thing?
        Buddha's preachings are for the living,
        nothing are they worth to the dead.
        But why do you hold me prisoner? Set me free!
Not yet. There is more I need to know.
Who were your parents, your mum and your dad?
        No mum, no dad, no siblings, reared all by myself.
Han-shan, I don't believe you are a man without a past.
Such simply don't exist.
Tell me where you came from!

>   A bird is not burderened by the remembrance
>   of once being an egg. It would drop from the sky.
>   Don't cut my wings off.
>   Nor does a butterfly know of its past
>   as a larva and a cocoon.
>   Let me flutter in peace, not in pieces.

You keep trying to evade me!
But at least you have now proven that you are still a poet.
Tell me then, what made you flee the lowlands?

>   I fled to get nearer to the moon.

Another poetic lie. I won't let you go before I have the truth.
Were you a slave, sold at a market,
that managed to escape?
Or was it the knife of the castrator
that drove you to this mountain so far away?
Did you fear to become a eunuch, or were you already one?
Shame or fear, I want to know!

>   What rudeness of you to ask like that.
>   What there is to know about me
>   is in the books you have on your shelves.

You know well they say nothing about your youth.
Every man has a past. And your ancestors,
how could you properly worship them,
far away from their tombs,
far away from your family temple?

>   In the world of spirits, there is no distance.
>   They were no nearer to me in the valley than on the slopes.
>   Could be I didn't show them the reverence I ought,
>   but at least I didn't treat them like you treat me.
>   And what business is it of yours to ask?

Han-shan, I need to know all about you.
Tell me now, who was Shih-te?

>   An echo, a shadow, never really alive.

So who wrote his poems?

>   I, mostly, and imitators.

And Feng-kan, how about him?

>   Just a village doctor, not worth to mention.
>   In the end, he was eaten by his tiger.

May it so go with you, if you don't set me free!
Thank you! But I am not over with you yet.
How many of the poems that are ascribed to you today
were actually written by you? Name them to me!
    So long ago, how could I remember?
    And what do you think I care?
    Words are but mumblings,
    faint echoes of the real world.
    The dead are beyond the vanity
    that makes people write and compose.
    Write your own poems, and leave mine alone!
So I will, even though I don't believe what you say.
But, Han-shan, you don't get my point:
I want to be you! That's why I pester you,
that is the whole and sole purpose of this grilling.
Han-shan, you are the only person I ever admired!
    In that case you should treat me better.
Correct. I'll let you go. Last question now. Tell me clearly:
Who are you and how did you get to be you?
    Through suffering we become what we are.
    Fate creates us, and you seem to me to be a man without a fate.
    Such people I detest. They are like spoiled children,
    never likely to create anything good.
    No chance have you got of becoming me,
    and little chance of coming to resemble me the slightest.
    This much, however, I'll tell you:
    To become like me, you have to give up everything,
    any ambition, any hope,
    the whole idea of becoming something,
    and, first of all, *you must give up the idea*
    of becoming me.

And with these words the scull went silent.
Not a word came from it, not a stir went through it.
Shamefully, I wrapped it up and returned it to the slopes
of that grey and barren mountain which bears its name.

ODD MAN

Odd man, this Han-shan.
He moved to a mountain
not to reach the top
but to reach a state
known as no-mountain.
Odd man indeed.

POETS IN DEBATE

Han-shan's been dead
for 1,300 years.
Where is he now?
Four poets are in debate.
First poet: I hear him in the wind.
Second poet: He's in the caw of the crow.
Third poet: He runs in my veins.
Fourth poet: He woke me up this morning.
His voice was in a jackhammer,
tearing up the street outside my door.
That's how they try to top each other.
Han-shan's surely been dead
for 1,300 years.

MONSOON

The monsoon has come,
bringing relief to the dried-out world.
Han-shan has left his leaking hut
to join the frogs in their praise.

QUESTIONS

Have you been wanking lately, Han-shan?
Does your cock ever point to the sky?
What do you think of when you masturbate
on that tall, cold mountain
where no woman ever sat her foot?

ASCENT

I climb the mountain
to get above the clouds
to clear my vision
to get where the real light shines.
The fog is lifting
and I look to the sky.
Is it the moon
hanging in that pine?
Or is it Han-shan's butt
pointing right at me?

THE SPIDER AND THE MOON

A giant spider has entangled the moon
in its web and locked it firmly
to the roots of Mount Han-shan.
The hare in the moon pounds nervously
in his mortar, thinking Han-shan will climb over
and steal his life-prolonging elixir.
Fear not, stupid hare! Han-shan is sound asleep
in his hammock. The moonlight injects him
with crazy dreams, and immortality is really
his least and very last care.

THE MERRY EXECUTIONERS

An execution took place the other day
in the Village of No-mind, at the foot of Mount Han-shan,
a dreadful scene, no sight for women and kids.
Ten men, at least, were beheaded, scoundrels,
bandits, finally caught after years of plunder and rape,
deserving no better fate than the one they got.
I know, 'cause I happened to pass by
when the scaffold was still dripping with blood,
severed, blood-smeared heads swayed high on stakes,
and headless corpses were being dragged away.
Who was the executioner? I asked an official.
I see the bodies and the scaffold, and there stands the axe,
but where is the man who swung it?
There were two, he said, they just ran off.
Two mountain hermits, caught by our men
when scavenging for food at our dump.
You see, those scoundrels that have just been beheaded
were all local men, known and feared by all,
some even had relatives among us.
Soldiers had caught them and brought them here for execution,
but we found no man willing to take upon him the task.
Some feared their *karma,* others the revenge of mortal men,
all were clever at finding excuses.
The mountain men were then brought in,
caught on suspicion of being thieves,
and had we had a headsman ready,
they would quickly have ended their days.
Fools they looked, and their clothes were in rags,
but smart enough they were to see in the mess
a chance for themselves to escape with their lives
and so humbly suggested we hand them the axe.
A deal was set; we agreed to grant them life and freedom,
would they but perform the headsman's task.
Not a moment did they waste.
Hardly had they been released from their ropes

before we saw them fighting over the axe.
And what a shock for us to see them in action,
chopping off heads with utmost delight,
cheerfully throwing them up in the air,
each time shouting *Ho!* and *Ha!*
and not minding themselves getting splashed with blood.
Were they men or demons, we wondered,
anxiously watching as their rude laughter filled the air
and heads were held up for people to behold.
Only a monk who came by was ready to praise them
for their lack of respect for death.
They are Buddhas in disguise, he whispered,
but he didn't dare to speak it out loud.
When finally the bloodshed was over,
and no more heads were waiting to be cut off,
their disappointment seemed as great as our relief.
Be glad you didn't witness this,
the official ended his story,
it was a ghastly, ghastly sight.
How much did you have to pay them? I wanted to know.
Not much, he replied, all that they asked for
was a thigh of the fattest robber,
a gift, they said, for their friend, a tiger,
and two severed heads
they wanted to use for pillows.
I saw them leave, laughing,
loudly praising their booty,
as they carried off their ghastly prizes
to those secret dwellings they call home,
and I thought to myself that with such people living
in our village, we'd never have to live in fear.
Yet I doubt that they'll ever return.
Who they were, we shall never know,
thus the man ended his tale,
but I remember the names that they used for themselves,
one was Han-shan, the other Shih-te,
and from the way they looked,
I couldn't tell one from the other.

DEATH OF HAN-SHAN

Grey clouds cover the mountain.
Is it day or night?
A mountain hermit tries to warm himself
by setting his own writings on fire.
Tomorrow he'll be dead,
his mind is already gone.
The fire is soon extinct
and the thin wane of smoke absorbed
by the frosty mist.

II. POEMS ASCRIBED TO HAN-SHAN

SHIH-TE

Shih-te has gone down in the valley, days ago,
after rice wine, but has not returned.
If I ever see the whore that snatched him,
I shall strangle her with my bare hands.

SHADOW

Standing on the southern slopes of Mount Han-shan,
exposing myself to the blinding sun,
does it alarm me
that I cast no shadow?

IN THE SNOW

The worst thing about winter
is that ice and snow cover everything.
There is not a bare rock
where I can carve my words.
I have to piss them
in the snow.

HAN-SHAN AND THE TIGER

The tiger is here,
scratching at my door,
wanting a share of my meal.
Alas! Stupid tiger! Don't you know
that Han-shan feeds only on herbs?
Bad tiger! Because of you
I made me a bow and an arrow of yew
and shot down the finest snub-nosed monkey
in the wood. Woe on me!
Serving meat to a tiger will surely ruin
my karma for a hundred years to come.

He eats and, having filled his stomach,
rolls over to me an arm
of the beautiful beast I just killed.
Evil tiger! You want me to share
with you that ghastly meal of yours?
Yet I cannot refuse
the polite invitation of a guest.
This is the first meat I've tasted
since long ago I was young.
My karma is ruined now
for a thousand years at least.

Han-shan burps, the tiger farts,
soon they are bundled up in sleep.
The stars are up,
the moon goes down,
soon even karma sleeps.

TOAD

A giant toad
crawls up the slopes of Mount Han-shan,
wanting to find Han-shan, the man,
and give him a venomous bite.
Crawl on, evil toad, but know
that Han-shan has fled to the moon.

GEOMETRY

Seen from the top of Mount Han-shan
the Earth forms a circle, so does the sky,
the sun and the moon.
Four circles and a mountain cone:
of these does the world consist.
I alone am here to watch it.
Sitting down, leaning my back against the mountain,
I let the circles perform
their slowly swirling, senseless dance.
The earth is red, the sky is blue,
the sun is yellow, white the moon.
How often does it not strike me
that I am alone in the world?

HAN-SHAN'S CAT (I)

When the cat washes itself
it expects visitors.
Clever cat I have
that never washes itself.

HAN-SHAN'S CAT (II)

My cat is the son of a tiger,
he claws the mice with ease.
Were you only bigger, cat,
you would eat old Han-shan too.

ORACLE BONES

The tiger's teeth
have transformed the skeleton of a goat
into oracle bones.
I pick up a shoulder blade
and try to decipher the inscription.
This tasted well, it reads,
but human meat would taste better.
Thank you, tiger,
for sending me this gentle warning.

TIGER SCRIPT

The tiger's claw
has left the sign for mountain
carved deep in my door.
Clever tiger, when you return,
I trust you have learned
to write my name in full.

HUSH!

The Buddhas of the past
and the Buddhas of the future
they've all come by to greet me.
I treat them with a stick
and feed their *sutras* to the fire.
Words contain no wisdom;
reserve them for the poets.
The true teachers are the wind,
the moon and the clouds.
How can you let them pass your door?
How can you chase them off?
Hush!

PERSPECTIVE

The raven belongs to the family of sparrows
and bamboo is technically a sort of grass.
I too have trouble figuring out
whether I'm a giant or a dwarf.

HAN-SHAN BLUES

The grass is crying
under the wind.
The hoofs of ten thousand horses
seem to be torturing it.
I guess one day I'll saddle the wind
and ride off to another land.

THE TORCH DRAGON

Having planned to watch the moon
on its steady course across the southern sky,
I am disturbed by the Torch Dragon
which flashes its green and blue band
on the northern sky.
I end up going early to bed
but my sleep is broken
by a string of uneasy dreams.
If the sky can't find rest,
how can a man?

WEIGHT

Even if I die
a thousand times
and am reborn each time
on this very spot,
the weight of my bodies
will add only little
to the strength of the mountain.
Rather do I fear
that the weight of my words
might make it crumble.
I guess I should praise the wind
for carrying them away.

CROW

Having your cliff writings edited
by the droppings of a bird
is really the last thing you need.
No wonder the crow is laughing so loud!
He has changed 'fire' to 'water'
and 'water' to 'ice'
and left the rest as a scribble.
Stupid bird! Tomorrow I'm gonna carve
my words deep in the rock
and the chisel I'll plant
right in your neck.

WHAT CAN BUDDHA TEACH THE RAIN?

What can Buddha
teach the rain?
Of what importance
is Boddhidharma to the snow?
Who says the wind
listens to Kung Fu Tse?
Will the sermons of Mo Tse
ever reach the moon?
And does the sun
prefer Chuang Tsu to Lao Tse?
I myself should stop
boring this old mountain
with my words.

HAN-SHAN'S CAT (III):

When thunder scares the cat
the mice run free.
In through a crack
comes the fattest rat,
having probably eaten
a lump of the moon,
and now seeking shelter
in the house of a frightened cat.

ENLIGHTENMENT

Why will the sun never reach enlightenment?
Because it doesn't need to.
And you—who ever told you
that you need to be anything else than what you are?

POND

This pond next to my hut,
with its singing frogs and buzzing insects,
with its mandarin ducks and weaver birds
nesting in the reeds,
and its bright surface reflecting the sky,
would I ever trade it
for the jade pool?

THREAT

Every day is the same.
I wake up, eat, piss and shit
and go to sleep.
That's all as it should be.
What worries me though
is that mountain of shit
with that river of piss
which threatens to reach the sky
and overshadow the real Han-shan.

EVENING

That sun going down sure looks like an apricot.
The sky is purple and packed with bats
and the moon, when it comes,
will likely be green.
The eerie call of a mountain monkey
has scared the cat out of its wits
and I must try and comfort Little Tiger.
I am drunk and should really get some sleep
but there's something I'm trying to remember:
Was it I who was named after the mountain
or was the mountain named after me?
My guess is I've simply been living here too long.

EXPOSED IN A DREAM

In a dream I was lost
in the depths of the bamboo forest
when a voice came to me and said:
It is too late to tear down
the mountain you have built.
The rest of the night I slept without dreams
but felt no comfort at all.

HAN-SHAN'S CAT (IV)

Nothing left to eat
but an onion
and the cat won't share
his mouse.

PERFECT DAY

Pissing in the river
attracts whales
and that line of clouds
looks like marching clowns.
What a perfect day
for doing nothing.

THE CLOUDS

Yang Zhu said, some thousand years ago,
that if he could save mankind
by pulling out a single hair from his head,
he would refrain.
If it was too much for him,
it is too much for me.
I spend my time watching the clouds
and it strikes me I'd be happy
to give all the hair on my head
if it could do them the slightest good.

ON MAKING AN END TO IT

Body of mine,
leave.
Walk out the door
and into the wood
where the tiger waits.
Have him assist you
in setting me free.

HAN-SHAN'S CAT (V)

The cat is smart,
has made his choice:
He's a cat.
I, however, can never make sure
whether I'm a cat or a mouse.

CLAY

Throwing clay in a clear pool
is considered bad.
Yet the result differs little
from sprinkling clear water upon clay.
If you meet a man of pure mind,
chase him off with a lump of clay.

KINGFISHERS

These two kingfishers have been fighting since early dawn
each trying to grasp the other by the beak
and hold him under water till he drowns.
How can so much evil thrive in such a pretty bird?
Watching them fight like that gets too much.
I draw back to get some rest.
When I return, late in the day,
blue and green feathers are floating in the brook.
One bird sits in triumph on a branch,
looking at the other, lying dead on the bank.

DREAMING OF SPRING

I dreamed there were fish in the brook.
I dreamed blue grass grew on the rocks.
I dreamed the snow had melted
and the heron had returned.
I dreamed I was no longer alone.

QIN

Shih-te plays the *qin*.
How gently his fingers move up and down the fretboard.
He plays *Wild Geese Landing on the Shore*
the way it was taught him by his father,
bringing back memories to us both
of our long lost youth in the lowlands.
Even with one string missing,
he manages to play the tune perfectly.
The whole hut reverberates
and the music penetrates the heavens.
Immortals congregate around him to listen
and outside in the thicket a cicada joins in.

SEARCHING FOR MOUNT HAN-SHAN

If you are searching for Mount Han-shan,
go elsewhere.
If someone says you've found it,
call him a liar.
If you see a hermit's hut,
clinging to the cliff like an eagle's nest,
be sure that the door won't open for you.
And if someone tells you you've reached the top,
you've surely lost your way.

NIGHT PICTURE

The wind, the moon, and the clouds,
the dark ink of the night,
of these things
does the world consist.
And then I shouldn't forget
the shrill shriek of an owl.

HAN-SHAN'S CAT (VI)

People say a tortoise-colored cat
is clever enough to predict earthquakes.
What a lie.
My cat was sound asleep
when Mount Han-shan shook its roots.

HAN-SHAN'S CAT (VII)

The cat has spent his day hunting butterflies,
now lies exhausted on his mat.
Spread on the floor
lie colorful wings of his victims.
Tell me truly, cat,
will you tonight be dreaming
of being a butterfly
hunting down frightened cats?

HAN-SHAN'S CAT (VIII)

Cat, what have you brought in?
The carcass of a rat.
An evil reminder of death,
or are you just trying to tell me
that my poetry stinks?

THANK THE FISH

Shih-te came by yesterday,
proud to tell he'd been fishing in the river
every day for six months without a catch,
a feat that brought him deep satisfaction.
Another six months like that,
and I'll be a perfect man, he declared.
This morning he went back to the river
and barely had he thrown out the line
before a salmon leapt right at the bait.
He quickly released it,
then went home in bitter disappointment,
swearing he'd never fish again.
Instead of blaming himself,
shouldn't he really be thanking the fish
for relieving him of the burden
of becoming a perfect man?

BALLS

I dreamt I was so big
that I could leap from one mountain peak to another.
People in the valley looked up in awe,
glaring at my giant balls.

EGG

Living on a mountain top,
surrounded by the endless sky,
does not prevent me from feeling locked up
in a tight and barren cell.
My poetry is all the same:
an egg described from inside.
How can I break the shell?
Not even death bears promise
of an easy escape.

IN SHIH-TE'S HUT

Shih-te has painted a cobweb on his ceiling
and has never since seen a fly.
The sign for cat on the door
helps mice and rats stay away,
and a broom, painted on the wall,
keeps his cottage clean.
Hunger is not his problem either,
since the word rice stands carved in his table.
Such is a true man of Dao.
Luckily, he has forgotten the character for wine,
so I still have an excuse
now and then to come by with a flask.

TO THE COURT POETS

What if I hate jade?
What if I find silk slick
and disgusting?
What if I don't like at all
the plick-plock sounds of the lute?
What if palaces are like prisons to me,
and what if I find your constant licking the ass
of emperors and courtiers
both desperate and humiliating,
directly speaking: unpoetic?
What else is then left of your art
than the pleasure of drinking,
the love of the moon,
and the joy of owls,
hooting in the night?
Which, after all,
is enough.

THE MOON AND THE EYE

The moon sinks in the water
and lets out a sea of blood.
Who stabbed it?
There is no one here
but me and my eye.

HARE

Winter is here, and the hare has once again changed his fur.
Come spring, and he'll put on his old grey suit.
The only hare that never changes color
is the one in the moon.
I know, 'cause I see him daily, year in and out,
pounding his mortarful of herbs.
Thank you, hare, for telling me
that there are no seasons
on the moon.

MISTY NIGHT

Don't waste this misty night
glaring at the moon.
There's a white rainbow behind you
and a white fox
jumping over a cup of wine.
A white maiden has poured it
and she awaits you
under a flowering elder.
Follow the track of the fox.
In this misty night
you are likely to get lost.

WORDS

With one word
you can strike like lightning.
Take ten words
to hit like a hammer.
Use a hundred words
to beat like a twig
and a thousand words
if you don't wish to strike at all.

RAT

This rat, feeding on a carcass,
looks at me with some kind of triumph,
mixed with fear.
Admire my catch, he seems to say,
but don't come to close.
Rat, you are disgusting,
and I'm ready to shower you with puke.
Only I fear you might take it
as a compliment.

FOOTPRINTS

A line of footprints from the village
tells of nightly visitors to the Kuo-Chi'ing temple.
No wonder the monks are busy shoveling snow.
Only women have such tiny feet.

THE WIND

Why does the wind always chase you
and why does he never fail to find you
no matter where you hide?
The wind wants something you have,
a prisoner, he says,
that you keep under lock
in a dark cage of ribs,
right next to your thumming heart,
and which he righteously claims to be his.
One day your cage will break open
and your prisoner escape.
That day you'll die
and the wind will at last reunite
with your breath.

SPIDER

This spider is another Buddha,
sitting in his finely spun pagoda,
promising the flies free entrance to Nirvana.
I call him abbot of the Kuo-Chi'ing temple.

TI-TSANG'S CHILDREN

Ti-tsang, Jizo to the Japanese,
protector of wayfarers and abortions,
has got his own corner at the graveyard
of the Kuo-Chi'ing temple, a mile or so from my hut.
A statue of him guards a moss-grown wall
with hundreds of tiny images engraved,
each representing the soul of a dead child.
Mothers come by daily to show their grief,
bringing offerings of wine and incense.
Monks stand by with pitiful faces,
waiting to take donations.
As night falls, the whimpering dies out.
The mourners go home
and the dead are finally left alone.

From time to time it happens then,
especially when the moon is up,
that a miniature procession starts out from the temple
and meanders up along the ridge to my hut.
It is the ghosts of abortions and stillborns
who wish to offer me the wine
that they themselves are unable to consume.
The shining line of torches approaching
and the chanting choir of weeny voices,
slowly filling the night
warn my cat that it is time to run off.
Rather seek the company of the tiger,
he seems to think, as he escapes into the dark,
just in time to avoid the spectral intruders.

My visitors bow politely as they enter,
hand me the wine, then sit down in a circle
and watch me as I drink,
each of them eager to tell his story.

Had we only had voices when we were alive,
one breaks the silence in a spooky whisper,
we could have screamed out our fear and anguish.
Many times it would have saved our lives.
And right he is. I've heard their stories before,
very similar they are,
and all of them equally gruesome.
I drink and listen without interrupting.
A quote from Chuang Tsu comes to my mind:
No one gets older than a dead infant,
but it is not likely to comfort them.
So on they go, through most of the night,
in voices their mothers never heard,
telling pathetic stories of bloodshed and terror,
now and then sticking out stumps and pointing at wounds,
as if their stories need additional proof.
With tears rolling, they accuse parents and priests,
doctors and officials; not even Buddha has been spared
when the final tale is told.
The more I drink, and the more I hear,
the more terrified I get.
Grown-ups scare me mostly with their lies.
Those little ones scare me with their truths.

Finally, when each has told his story
and only drops of wine are left,
they get on their feet to leave.
Politely they excuse me for taking my time
and express the hope that I will allow them in again
another time. And of course I will.
For a while I watch them from the door
as they parade down the slope,
staggering, as if as drunk as I.
When the last one has disappeared,
the cat returns and we both go to sleep,
facing some hours of tense and troubled dreams.

Morning comes with a knock on my door.
Shih-te walks in, finding me not fully awake.
Who got you drunk? he asks,
but I won't reply.
The truth is often too much like a lie.
Even my best friend will hardly believe me.
I prefer it to remain a secret,
shared by me and my cat.

SHIH-TE BOWS OUT

Shih-te has plucked down the moon,
wiped it with his sleeve,
and stuck it up his nose.
He has uprooted most of the forest
and placed it on his brow.
Birds are nesting in his hair,
and I hear monkeys bellow from his beard.
The brook, which I loved, is now dripping from his lips
and the mountain itself, he has folded
and saved as a biscuit under his tongue.
Thus equipped, he can hardly speak.
He's outside my door, knocking hard,
but I won't let him in,
having guessed what he wants.
The tiger has escaped him,
and he's here to collect my cat.
My old friend is getting ready
to leave this world behind.

SHIH-TE'S DEATH

Shih-te is dead. The raven fondly kisses
his body, spread out in the snow.
I watch from a distance and regret
that I, his friend,
cannot show him the same affection.
That's how death
separates friends.

TROUBLE

Worse than being hungry
and having nothing to eat
is to shit and have nothing
with which to wipe your ass.
No moss at hand, no leaves,
no bamboo scraper.
Cannot use the sacred scrolls
belonging to the temple,
willnot use my scribblings,
useless as they may be.
If only the cat would come by,
I'd grab him by the neck.
Kitty! Kitty!

HUT AND CASTLE

This hut may not seem much
with its leaking roof and crumbling walls,
but inside, in a corner, under a rotten beam,
a spider resides in a castle.

END OF MOUNT HAN-SHAN

If this mountain went up in flames
I would end as a wisp of smoke
and would it worry me?
If the mountain froze
I would end as an ice crystal
and would it worry me?
If the mountain melted
I would end as a cold water stream
and would it worry me?
If the mountain dried out
I would end as a frowning rock
and would it worry me the least?

RESPONSE

The evening trumpet of the Kuo-Chi'ing temple
sets a bull roaring in the valley,
and from the bamboo grove
an old monkey bellows in response.
Buddha has followers everywhere.
I turn my face to the sky,
awaiting an echo from the moon.

MOSQUITOS

The mosquitos are happy today, Shih-te announces.
We are both standing in a buzzing cloud of insects.
How do you know they're happy, I ask,
you're not an insect, so how can you tell?
My friend laughs overbearingly: It's easy.
I can tell by the itching of my arm.

AGEING

Getting deaf
fearing my own mirror image
skin getting scaly
nails looking like claws
tomorrow waking up
as a dragon.

COW AND ABBOT

I've come to respect the abbot.
He boasted of knowing the sutras by heart
and I asked, can he teach a cow to piss?
Abbot said, bring me a cow.
Cow came; the abbot kicked it in the ****
—and boy, could that cow piss!

TIGER TRAP

The wind has collapsed the bamboo forest
and left it as a giant tiger trap.
Broken stems stand like spears,
birds and squirrels are left homeless.
Only with the greatest caution
dare I venture into this ruined jungle.
My eyes are on a bird nest, full of youngs,
knocked down by hail and wind,
and abandoned by the mournful parents.
I pick it up and hide it in my sleeve.
Is my plan to save those little ones from the marten
or have I in mind to present them to my cat?
On my way out, I spike my foot
and limping, decide to leave the nest behind.

BOWL

An insect crawling in a bowl,
trying to get out—
that's life in the valley.
An insect crawling on the outside
of a reversed bowl,
trying to get in—
that's life on the mountain.
Why don't I just flee to the moon?

MELTING SNOW

Melting snow
reveals last autumn's scribblings
on the cliffs.
So full of errors,
so shakingly written,
they resemble the work of a child.
Deeply ashamed, I have to pray for spring
to come late.

MEASURING THE MOUNTAIN

Mount Han-shan measures 4,500 feet.
Not much of a mountain, people say,
why don't I move to another?
I tell them I don't need a mountain
that won't fit into my sleeve.

ISOLATION

Having isolated myself on this desolate spot,
it is not the lack of friends that worries me
but that of enemies.
I should go back to the lowlands,
pick up a sword
and cut somebody down.

SPEAKING TO THE DEAD

Why go to the graveyard
to speak to the dead
when the tiger's cave is so much nearer
and sculls and bones are exposed all over the floor?

CATCH A CLOUD

Catch a cloud and chain the sky.
Dry the rain and pull the river back.
Bridle the wind and stop the moon.
Mute the thunder, put the low of the cow
back in the throat of the beast.
When this is done, go and tame yourself.

MOON

Today's work at the Kuo-Chi'ing temple is over,
and my broom is set aside.
Eager to return to my hut,
I begin looking for Shih-te.
I find him in the kitchen,
busy reminding a blind monk
not to miss tonight's moon.

SOMETHING THAT LOOKS LIKE A COW

Something that looks like a cow has entered my hut.
It has two big horns and a silly face -
but is it a cow?
In this world of illusions, you can never be sure.
Underneath its belly I find an udder with four teats.
It could well be a cow - at least it's not a woman!
But can it produce milk?
I pull a handle, and yes! Milk comes out.
I would certainly call it a cow.
Then suddenly, on the floor,
the evidence: a pat!
The biggest one I ever saw.
As Lord Buddha said:
From the dung you can tell the beast.
It *is* a cow.
But what good can the knowledge do me?
It just ate my favourite scroll.

MOSS

Gathering moss for the temple loo,
that's how I make my bread.
A bag of moss for a loaf of bread,
that's what they call mountain economy.
Down on all fours, cutting moss in slices,
carefully removing every twig and thorn,
wiping off insects and slugs
so they won't get stuck in the abbot's ***,
what a pleasant way to spend the day!
Never in a hurry, I take my time to study
the microworld I'm about to destroy.
Could they speak, these little ones,
they'd tell stories of a world like ours,
of emperors and heroes, of poets
and of dragons fierce,
known to us as scorpions and snakes,
and posing a danger even to me.
A praying mantis is a reborn abbot,
ants are like soldiers,
marching through the fields,
all sorts of people do I meet in disguise.
Ugly bugs are courtiers, eunuchs,
never did I like their kind.
Butterflies are pretty women,
cicadas their musicians,
moths perhaps their kind of ghosts,
and that spider throning in his web
resembles well the emperor,
residing in his castle.
All are they about to meet an equal fate
as I root up their world
and hide it in my bag.
If their world resembles ours so closely,
then ours must resemble a bigger one,
that of the gods, I guess,

and we are all in imminent danger
of being uprooted and ending up stuck
in some divinity's ass.
This is the kind of wisdom I get
from daily gathering moss.
The monks regard me as a fool
and smile when I deliver my harvest.
Sitting in the loo, wiping their asses,
they don't waste a thought on me,
but what do I care?
And when people from the valley come by
and ask: What brought you here?
How do you spend your time?
I answer them truly, without telling a lie:
I came here to study the wisdom of moss.

IMAGINING HIS LAST POEM

As a young man
I knew well over 5,000 characters
and wrote them flawlessly.
I dare say few modern scholars
can claim anything near that.
And how beautiful my was handwriting then!
Today, aged, my hand is shaking,
and I remember barely 400 signs.
At least one can say
that my poetry has become very concise.
If this continues
my last poem will soon write itself
and consist of the last three words I remember.
I hope it will sound like this:

MAN – MOON – MOUNTAIN

WIND AT THE DOOR

The wind is out, chasing ghosts.
He's at my door now,
trying out every crack.
What's on your mind,
stupid wind?
I am alone in my hut
and I ain't no ghost.

HAN-SHAN'S JISEI

Death has knocked on my door.
Finally it's time to leave this old body behind.
Goodbye, farting machine.
Goodbye, piss pot.
Goodbye, shit processor.
Goodbye, screwing automaton.
Goodbye, food grinder.
Goodbye.

APPENDIX I: BONE AND MARROW

Moving in circles,
every exile is a return to home.

A Buddha in a whorehouse
remains a Buddha
in a whorehouse.

Wiping your ass with the holy scriptures -
will it get you or your asshole to Nirvana?

Mocking the moon is a waste of time.
But still - look at its stupid face!

The door to my hut opens either way
so that even the tiger can find his way in.

The more I look at people
the more I appreciate the company of my cat.

Glaring at the moon
won't take you there.
And yet.

Licking a toad's skin
and soon after
seeing two moons.

If this is a world of suffering
how is it that I feel so at ease?

Clouds are like people drifting by.
Would you ever ask one to pause?

Living in accordance with the Way is easy
when you have no neighbors.

True saints live in crowded houses.

Why is it that every time I look into this pond
a warted toad looks back?

A flying bird leaves no traces.
So what was it that just hit me
on the head?

Mysticism is just another word for laziness,
said the abbot.
I guess that makes me the biggest mystic ever.

Over the hillocks -
same moon, same clouds.

Is it because I shat behind this thicket
that a blooming rose has shot up?

In a world of crashing boulders
who needs egos? who needs souls?

APPENDIX II: HAN-SHAN'S PROVERBS

A blind archer may hit the moon.

Chase out the spider and have your house filled with flies.

In the company of Buddhas nothing but boredom.

You have to dig deep if you plan to bury the moon.

Easy as picking up snakes.

Silk will burn your skin. If not now, then in hell.

A single fart will raise dust on the moon.

With a serpent in your bed, no need to fear the rats.

Between a snorting dragon and a roaring tiger, what sense does it make to raise your voice?

An arrow shot at the sun is an arrow lost. An arrow shot at the moon is an arrow in your neck.

Pulling the arrow out of the wound may kill you.

Feeding meat to a tiger, do not worry for your karma.

When trying to shoot down the moon, don't aim too carefully.

Water your mud ox, but don't water it too well.

Glaring at the night sky won't bring the new moon up.

Each man in his own skin.

When out of ink use your blood.

NOTES

The subtitle; the detective reader will notice that the numbers of poems indicated are incorrect; I am here in full accordance with Japanese, and possible also Chinese tradition.

p. 13 broom; Han-shan's tool and attribute
p. 14 koan; in Zen Buddhism, an unsolvable riddle, meant to trigger enlightenment
p. 16 Po Chü-i; a leading T'ang poet
p. 16 Fa Ch'ang; a Chinese ink artist
p. 16 Chuang Tsu; one of the founders of Daoism
p. 18 Jack Kerouac; dedicated his book, *Dharma Bums*, to Han-shan
p. 19 the Book of Changes; the oracle book also known as *I Ching*
p. 19 stalks of milfoil; remedies for divination
p. 21 QUESTIONING HAN-SHAN'S SCULL; inspired by Chang Heng's poem *The Bones of Chuang Tzu,* translated by Arthur Waley
p. 23 Shih-te; Han-shan's friend, usually depicted as a look-alike. The name means 'pick-up' and is believed to refer to him as a foundling
p. 23 Feng-kan; another friend of Han-shan, often depicted with a tame tiger. His name means 'big stick', not referring to what you think, but to his long walking staff
p. 26 the hare in the moon; the Chinese myth of a hare pounding immortality elixir on the moon probably derives from an ancient interpretation of the contours on the moon
p. 33 not a bare rock; Han-shan reportedly wrote his poems on cliffs and carved them in trees
p. 36 oracle bones; cracks and scratches in animal bones were interpreted as messages from the spirits
p. 37 PERSPECTIVE; the poem is anachronistic, since both the classification of ravens as sparrows, and of bamboo as grass belong to a much later day than that of Han-shan. So why not leave it out? Because a good book should contain errors
p. 38 the Torch Dragon; a sky phenomenon. In *The Classic of Mountains and Seas,* a book that predates the Christian era, the term is used in a way that gives no clues as to its exact meaning. In another ancient anthology, *The Songs of the South,* which probably dates from the second century A.D., the

term almost certainly refers to northern lights, a rare but not impossible phenomenon at Mount Han-shan's latitude

p. 39 Boddhidharma; legendary founder of Zen Buddhism

p. 39 Kung Fu Tse; founder of Confucianism

p. 39 Mo Tse; Chinese philosopher

p. 39 Lao Tse; legendary founder of Daoism

p. 40 enlightenment; a Buddhist concept

p. 40 the jade pool; an attraction in the Chinese paradise

p. 43 Yang Zhu; an elusive Chinese philosopher, probably from the third century B.C. The only statement from him I have found is that really arrogant one about refusing to save mankind even by something as simple as pulling out a hair of your own head. I probably understand it in a different way from how it was meant. Don't bother consulting the Yang Zhu chapters in Lie Tse; they are later constructions of no authenticity

p. 44 man of pure mind; a Daoist concept

p. 44 blue grass; both in Japan and China, grass is considered blue. The conception may go back to really ancient times when the language was not fully developed and all color variations had not yet been given names

p. 45 qin; a Chinese four-string harp

p. 45 *Wild Geese Landing on the Shore;* a classic composition for qin, dating back at least to the fifth century

p. 45 immortals; a Daoist concept

p. 47 perfect man; a Daoist ideal. Han-shan could himself be taken for one, but definitely wouldn't wish to be so

p. 49 joy of owls; owls, favorite birds of mine, were actually thought ominous. See note to p. 37

p. 51 Kuo-Chi'ing temple; where Han-shan worked as a kitchen hand

p. 53 Ti-tsang; there are Ti-tsang and Jizo shrines like here described, but not at the Kuo-Chi'ing temple

p. 57 MOSQUITOS; as the bright reader will notice, this poem is but a merry duplication of one of Chuang Tsu's parables

p. 58 being deaf, fearing one's mirror image, being scaly and having nails like claws; all characteristics of the Chinese dragon

p. 61 From the dung you can tell the beast; Lord Buddha never said anything remotely like this

p. 65 jisei; death poem. Actually a Japanese concept

p. 68 mud ox; illusions. A Zen concept

www.ingramcontent.com/pod-product-compliance
Lightning Source LLC
Chambersburg PA
CBHW031420040426
42444CB00005B/655